GRANDMA MOSES

GRANDMA MOSES

MARGOT CLEARY

BISON GROUP

First published in 1991 by
Bison Books Ltd.
Kimbolton House
117A Fulham Road
London SW3 6RL

ISBN 0 86124 824 4

Printed in Hong Kong

Page 1:
The Checkered House, 1943. Oil
on canvas, 36×45 in. K 317

Page 2:
Pumpkins, 1959. Oil on pressed
wood, 16×24 in. K 1380

Right:
The Marsh, 1951-52. Tile 51,
6×6 in.

Far Right:
Playing, 1951-52. Tile 35, 6×6
in.

CONTENTS

INTRODUCTION

Left: Grandma Moses in her studio. She was 92 when this picture was taken.

Far right: Anna Mary Robertson, the future Grandma Moses, when she was a girl of 15.

Right below: Anna Mary at the age of 4.

Anna Mary Robertson Moses was to become famous as Grandma Moses when she was in her 80s, some decades after she had first dug some old paints out of her barn and began recording the American country scenes that she knew so well. But sudden though her fame was, it was a lifetime in the making: a lifetime of hard, satisfying work by a woman with a sense of humor and a keen eye for the details of everyday life. "Memory is history recorded in our brain," she once observed. "Memory is a painter . . . ."

Anna Mary Robertson started out a farm girl and stayed a farm girl until the end of her days. She was born on September 7, 1860, in the hills of upstate New York near the Vermont border, to Russell King Robertson, a farmer who grew flax, and Mary Shannahan Robertson. One of 10 children, Anna Mary spent her early years learning how to do women's work on the farm. She helped raise the younger children, made soap and candles and boiled down maple sap. But even as a young girl she had an eye for what she thought was pretty and pleasing: apple blossoms in spring, a glistening mound of soap suds, the bright colors of the cotton fabrics the peddler brought on his visits to the Robertson farm.

In her free time, Anna Mary would often race about with her brothers, rafting on the mill pond or speeding down snowy hills on home-made sleds. Or sometimes she would spend hours making clothes for her paper dolls, fashioning little outfits from old envelopes or newspapers or, if she had managed to charm the peddler, some bits and pieces of colorful cloth.

At other times she would busy herself making pictures. Her father, who had done some painting himself, would bring home sheets of newsprint now and then ("It was a penny a sheet and

it lasted longer than candy," Anna Mary figured) and she would set to work. First she would draw in her design, then find her "paints" – some berry juice, perhaps, or a stick or two of carpenter's chalk – and color them as prettily as she could. Soon Anna Mary was painting on old bits of wood, glass and slate. Her brothers poked fun at her "lambscapes," as she called them, but her father urged her on: "Not so bad," he would say. Mrs Robertson, however, was of a more practical bent: in her view, Anna Mary's time would be better spent in work around the house.

She went to school for just a few months of each year (she was especially fond of geography because she got to draw maps in class), and the rest of her year was spent helping out at home. She learned to sew and to cook, and by the time she was 12 Anna Mary was ready to leave home and earn her keep as a hired girl. "Those happy days" of childhood were over, she wrote much later. "Then began the hard years."

Her first job was with an elderly couple who came to look on Anna Mary as their own daughter, and before long she came to feel as if she were. She took over the household chores – doing up the wash, making and mending the clothes, tending the garden and, best of all from her point of view, doing the cooking. She especially liked it when the couple had guests and she could prepare meals of cured beef with biscuits, butter and honey, and serve them on the household's best china and linens.

When that couple no longer needed her services Anna Mary went on to a job with another family, and after that, still another. Yet there were reassuring constants in life in the country that helped to ease the disruptions of moving. There were the Sunday trips to church, for example, where the socializing was almost as important as the worship, and the country fairs of late summer and fall, where farm families could proudly display the fruits of their labors.

In 1886 Anna Mary moved on to yet another family, but this job would prove to be a turning point in her life. The hired man on the farm was a Thomas Salmon Moses, and over time he and Anna Mary grew fond of each other. He appreciated her cooking; she appreciated his good nature and thrifty ways. By now she was in her mid-20s, and she knew what was important in a man: "Some kinds of women like a man because he is rich," she wrote half a century later, "but that kind of like is not lasting, just lasts as long as the pocketbook." Anna Mary and Thomas were married in November 1887, with the bride wearing a dark green dress and a matching hat adorned with a pink feather. She knew from the start what kind of marriage she wanted to have. "I believed, when we started out, that we were a team and I had to do as much as my husband did, not like some girls, they sit down, and then somebody has to throw sugar at them. I was always striving to do my share."

The couple decided to strike out on their own. Thomas had learned of a farm in North Carolina that might need someone to run it, and soon after their wedding they said goodbye to their relatives in New York and headed south. But on the way, an overnight stop in the Shenandoah Valley changed their plans: they were so taken by the beauty of the spot and the

friendliness of the people that they hired on to run a small farm in the town of Staunton, Virginia. Barely married a month, Anna Mary later reflected, they had found a new home, in a new land, with new people: "Now we were in the swim – it was paddle or sink!"

They wasted no time in settling in. Anna Mary got herself a flock of hens ("They are lots of care but good company") and helped Thomas plant the crops and milk the cows. Before long Mrs. Moses began to get a reputation in the Valley for her butter. Yankee butter, the locals called it, and it was so tasty that soon it was selling for two and a half times the price of locally-produced butter. In just a few months Anna Mary's butter earned her enough money to pay for two cows.

With Anna Mary's reputation as the region's best butter-maker established, the Moseses were offered a job running a 600-acre dairy farm near Fort Defiance, Virginia: the owner told them he would pay them more than the going rate for all the butter they could produce. Thomas had a butter mold made up with the name "Moses" imprinted on it and sent North for a barrel churn so that his wife could make each day's butter in one big batch.

Just a little more than a year after their marriage the couple had their first baby, Winona. Anna Mary worked right through her pregnancy – there was no time for leisure – and was back at work just nine days after the birth. More children followed quickly; the Moseses would have 10 in all, although five would die at birth or shortly after. But even a growing family did not

Left: Anna Mary Moses in 1904, with her son Hugh and her daughter Anna.

Right: From left to right, Winona, Forrest and Loyd, the three oldest children of Grandma Moses.

stop Anna Mary from doing her share of work on the farm. In any case, she conceded, hers were easy childreen: "I didn't bring up the children, they kind of come up."

When the owner of the dairy farm died, the family moved on to another farm nearer Staunton. It was here that the Moseses' foray into the butter business ended; this was strictly a milking operation. The hours Anna Mary had spent at the churn were now devoted to washing out milk bottles, more than a hundred each day, and it was no easy task: she had to haul wood and water for all that washing up 17 stairs. Still, she recalled late in her life, she had never minded it. "Hard work, but it was very nice."

The Moses family moved around the Shenandoah Valley to several more farms after that, and as always, Anna Mary was more than busy, growing and selling her vegetables or cooking up apple butter 40 gallons at a time. The cooking skills that had first endeared her to Thomas were better than ever, and soon her canned fruits and vegetables were winning prizes at country fairs.

The Moses family had been settled down South for nearly 20 years, and Anna Mary had come to think of the Shenandoah Valley as home. But Thomas had grown homesick for New York, so in 1905 they went back north, hiring a railroad car to bring back not just their furniture and household goods but an assortment of produce and livestock as well. Once back at her parents' home Anna Mary decided little had changed in the time she and Thomas had been gone – even the hinge on the

gate still needed repair, just as it had when she had left home nearly two decades earlier.

The Moseses soon bought a farm in Eagle Bridge, New York, and settled into a comfortable routine not much different from their life in Virginia. Anna Mary spent the beginning of each week doing the washing and ironing. Mid-week was reserved for baking, with the weekend devoted to sewing and gardening. For excitement the family went to picnics, fairs and, occasionally, the circus. It was a steady, peaceful, largely uneventful life.

Anna Mary's childhood attempts at painting pretty pictures were just a memory for most of these years; her work on the farm left her no time for "frivolous" activities. Not surprisingly, then, it was necessity that got her painting again.

It was 1918, and Anna Mary was busy wallpapering the parlor of the house in Eagle Bridge when she ran out of paper for the fireboard. She knew she needed to fill the space with something, so she pasted black paper over the board, found some brushes and paints and got to work painting in trees, a lake with the sun reflecting off it and some bushes in the foreground. That fireboard landscape was her first big picture, Anna Mary said later. But while she was proud of her effort it was just a means to an end; later she would paper over her painted fireboard. Yet, she had enjoyed making the picture, and now and then she would take up a brush again and paint little pictures to give to her family and friends.

In 1927, 40 years after marrying Anna Mary Robertson,

Thomas Moses caught a cold going out to fetch wood; he died of heart failure a few hours later. His death was a painful shock to Anna Mary, for Thomas had always been in good health. But she *had* noticed one change in him shortly before his death. Always before he had regarded her attempts at painting as "foolish," but toward the end something had been different; he would watch her paint and admire what she did. Years later, when her career as an artist was in full bloom, Anna Mary would wonder if her success was in some way her husband's doing. "I am not superstitious or anything like that. But there is something like an overruling power . . . It was just as though he had something to do about this painting business."

"This painting business" would not, however, get underway for a few more years. After her husband's death Anna Mary's son and daughter-in-law took on much of the work of the farm, and while Anna Mary continued to help out – she could not bear the thought of sitting idle – she finally had a bit of time for herself. Her eye for color and design, for making pretty things, had not been lost on the family, and her daughter urged her to make some worsted wool embroidered pictures such as those sometimes seen at local fairs. Anna Mary tried this "fancy

work" and found she was good at it: she eventually crafted more than 50 of the worsted pictures, using bright yarns to create scenes she knew well – a sunset in the Shenandoah Valley, a covered bridge in New York, the woods in winter. She gave most of these pictures away as gifts.

By the time she had reached her 70s Anna Mary was beginning to feel the effects of rheumatism. A concoction of milk and turpentine took care of the pain, but her fingers were no longer nimble enough to manage the needle and threads for her worsted pictures. Her sister urged her to pick up a paint brush again. "So I did," Anna Mary recalled, "and painted for pleasure, to keep busy and to pass the time away, but I thought of it no more than of doing fancy work." She would get some scraps of hard masonite board, hunt for an old frame in the attic, assemble some paints bought from Sears and set to work. Sometimes she pulled out the collection of pictures she had cut out of calendars and magazines and greeting cards over the years and try to copy them, always adding her own touches. For other pictures she relied on her own memories of the places she had lived. And sometimes she would imagine scenes from stories that had been passed down in the family, such as the one about the covered wagon, built by one of her ancestors, that had been the first to travel the local turnpike. She painted the patchwork fields of the valley where she lived; the mill that her father had run long ago; cows grazing in the Shenandoah Valley; a sugaring-off scene in late winter. Her pictures were filled with striking colors and an abundance of detail, plus a strong narrative element.

The pictures were good, her family told her, so she entered a few in a local fair, along with some of her canned goods. The fruits and jams won a prize, but not the paintings. Yet she was undismayed; she was, after all, painting for her own pleasure. Work was its own reward, as it had always been for her.

Anna Mary was as industrious about her painting as about everything else in her life, and before long she had a considerable collection of pictures. Why don't you take them down to Thomas' Drugstore? someone asked; the owner is organizing an exchange for work done by local women. Anna Mary went along with the idea, more than likely without giving it much thought. But that little "exhibit" at Thomas' drugstore in Hoosick Falls, New York, in the late 1930s would eventually change her life.

The pictures languished in the drugstore window for nearly a year. Then, in 1938, an art collector from New York City, Louis Caldor, who was taking a ride through the country, stopped by Thomas' store. Caldor was so taken with Anna Mary's paintings that he bought every one of them on the spot and then headed for her home, hoping to find more. The artist happened to be out, but when she got home that night her daughter-in-law, Dorothy, told her that Caldor had been ready to buy every painting she had. He would be back in the morning, Dorothy said, adding that she had told him her mother-in-law probably had another 10 paintings around the house.

Anna Mary spent a restless night, wondering if she could come up with that many more paintings. By morning she had found only nine. But she was nothing if not practical , so she simply took out her scissors and cut one of the biggest paintings in half.

Caldor bought all 10 (or nine – it was some time before he realized that two of the paintings had once been one) and took them back to New York, sure that he had made the artistic find of the decade. He spent months carting the pictures around in his car from gallery to gallery, trying to generate interest in them. Many of the people he contacted agreed that the paintings were nice, but, they told Caldor, they were looking for contemporary themes and styles, not rural scenes of days gone by. Besides, the artist was nearly 80, not a good bet for a long-lived career.

Still Caldor persevered. In 1939 he heard about an upcoming show at the Museum of Modern Art in New York that was to be devoted to "Contemporary Unknown American Painters."

Left: The farm at Eagle Bridge, New York, where Thomas and Anna Mary Moses made their home in 1905.

Right: Grandma Moses with her painting "Down on the Farm" in 1945.

Anna Mary Moses was all of those, certainly, and her paintings fit the "primitive" style the museum was promoting: highly decorative and colorful works by untrained artists, with a strong sense of narrative. Caldor persuaded the show's organizer to include three of her paintings: "Home," "In the Maple Sugar Days" and "The First Automobile." At last there was a glimpse of recognition, but the show did not succeed in sparking any wide-scale interest in Anna Mary's works, and the three paintings were returned to Caldor after it closed.

He continued to stay in touch with Anna Mary, sending her some artists' paints and urging her to keep working. But in fact he was getting nowhere in his efforts to gain an audience for his "discovery." More months went by, and then Caldor made the acquaintance of a cultivated Austrian refugee from Naziism who had just opened a gallery in New York. In Vienna and Paris, Otto Kallir had specialized in dealing in modern paintings, but he had a taste for folk art as well and agreed to take a

look at the work of the old woman on the farm.

Kallir dismissed some paintings out of hand – mostly the ones that had obviously been copied from Anna Mary's stack of clippings – but others struck him with their sense of design, their liveliness and what Kallir recognized as their "simplicity and candor." The artist, he realized, had an unusual talent for observing what was around her. Her titles indicated what she felt the true subject of each painting was (often just a detail tucked away in some part of a scene), and Kallir knew that her involvement with what she painted was intensely personal: "Whether the picture was of a washday or a Sunday, it was her washday, her Sunday." They were highly personal works, yet they were so lively and spontaneous that a viewer could not help being drawn into them.

Caldor's faith in Anna Mary Moses was finally vindicated. Kallir said that he would give her a solo show – as long as he could select the paintings. "What A Farm Wife Painted"

Left: Grandma Moses at work in her Eagle Bridge home in 1955, just days before her 95th birthday.

Right: The exterior and garden of Grandma Moses' house in Eagle Bridge, both familiar subjects in her paintings.

opened at the Galerie St. Etienne on 57th Street in New York on October 8, 1940. The show consisted of 34 paintings, most of them quite small, with names like "Bringing in the Hay" and "In the Maple Sugar Days." There was no catalogue, just a mimeographed sheet of the titles. Anna Mary decided not to go to the show; after all, she had already seen all of the paintings, so what was the point?

The exhibit garnered some good reviews from art critics, but there was no rush to buy Anna Mary's work. Of the 34 paintings, priced between $20 and $250, only three found buyers. But though it may not have been a financial success, the show did succeed in making a name for Anna Mary Moses. One newspaper article noted that the artist was known locally as "Grandma Moses," and Grandma Moses she was to be from then on. The public quickly took to her, fascinated not only by her paintings of a way of life that held great appeal in increasingly complicated times, but also by the story of a hard-

working, no-frills farm wife who had not had the leisure to paint seriously until she was nearly 80. Grandma Moses was living proof of the old adage, "It's never too late."

Gimbels department store in New York wasted no time in arranging an exhibit of Grandma Moses' works for its Thanksgiving season, and it asked the artist to come to New York to speak. This time she accepted the invitation and headed for the city accompanied by Carolyn Thomas, the owner of the Hoosick Falls drugstore that had first displayed her paintings. Grandma Moses had only been to the "big city," as she called it, a handful of times in her life, and she was somewhat taken aback by the crowds of people who showed up to hear her. But Louis Caldor had foreseen the situation and advised her to bring along some of her jams and home-baked breads, in case she wanted to speak a bit about those as well as her paintings. And, after finding herself hooked up to a microphone and seated on a stage next to Mrs. Thomas, that is exactly what

Grandma Moses ended up doing. Later, she remembered her dilemma this way: "They took me by surprise. I was in from the back woods, and I didn't know what they were up to. So while I thought I was talking to Mrs. Thomas, I spoke to 400 people at the Thanksgiving Forum in Gimbels' auditorium." Her audience left well-versed in the secrets of good home cooking, and utterly charmed by the tiny, white-haired woman and her down-to-earth manner. Straightforward, hard-working and good-natured, with just enough of a tart tongue to save her from being saccharine, Grandma Moses was on her way to becoming a folk heroine.

Most art-world opinion-makers still continued to dismiss her paintings as unsophisticated exercises in nostalgia, little more than sentimental longings for the good old days. But not for long. The attention her pictures were attracting had inspired Grandma Moses to work hard at them, as she had worked at everything else in her life, and soon her paintings were showing a new freedom. She used color more inventively, blending it in new ways and adding depth to her paintings. She was also using better, more professional materials – real artists' paints and brushes, instead of cast-offs from barn and attic. Her subjects were still simple, but Grandma Moses' sophistication as a painter was growing rapidly.

The general public was eager to see more of her work. Her paintings of holiday celebrations and family gatherings, of country villages and rural acres, of the constants of work and play, were universal images that struck a chord in people everywhere. In quick succession Grandma Moses had shows in Washington, DC, and Syracuse, New York, and her painting entitled "The Old Oaken Bucket" won The New York State Prize in 1941. By the time her paintings were exhibited at another New York gallery in 1942, her work had become so much more accomplished that the formal art world had no choice but to take notice.

As respect for her work grew, so did demand. Before long Grandma Moses was getting "orders" for paintings from people who wanted a picture just like one of those they had seen reproduced in the by-now burgeoning publicity about the artist. When they asked about price, Grandma Moses would reply, "Well, how big a picture do you want?" Smaller picturers as she saw it, should cost less, since they used up less paint. Business was brisk, and for a time Grandma Moses painted assembly-line style. She would set three or four pieces of masonite side by side, sketch in the outlines with pencil, then paint in all the skies, all the hills and so on. Once the basic painting had taken shape, she would add the details that made each work distinct.

While her technique was growing more sophisticated the actual progress of painting for Grandma Moses was as straightforward as the woman. For her easel she used a small tip-up table that had once been a flower stand; in 1920 she had prettied it up by painting scenes of rivers, hills and valleys on the sides and pasting postcards on the top. She painted in her bedroom and had to paint her biggest pictures on her bed, since the tip-up table was too small. Otto Kallir had often asked to watch Grandma Moses at work and could never understand why she refused until she explained to him that it just wasn't proper for a man to enter her bedroom.

Her first task, when she got ready to paint, was to find a frame. That was the sensible way to go about it, she said, adding "I always thought it a good idea to build the sty before getting the pig." Next she would cut a piece of masonite to fit. She liked masonite because it lasted longer than canvas, an important consideration to someone who prided herself on her Scottish thrift. Then, sitting on a chair supplemented by a

Left: Grandma in Eagle Bridge in 1948 rehearsing for a remote TV interview in which she will respond to questions posed by art critics in New York City.

Sears catalog and an old Bible to give her a boost, she would begin to paint.

She began by priming the board with linseed oil and three coats of white paint for "body," so she would not have to use as much of the more expensive colored paints. (The white base had the added advantage of giving her paintings a luminous quality.) Then she would stop to think about just what it was she wanted to paint that day – perhaps a famous local landmark, or a winter scene, or the peach blossoms just showing on some distant hills. Whatever she fixed upon, however, there was one constant: "Always something pleasing and cheerful, I like bright colors and activity."

Demand for the paintings was soon so strong that it became apparent that, industrious as Grandma Moses was, she could never hope to meet it. The first of a series of reproductions were therefore made available, bringing Grandma Moses' work to a larger audience. An even broader public was reached when Hallmark Cards, Inc., bought the rights to reproduce a number of her paintings. Grandma Moses' originals were now commanding sizeable sums in the art market, and her arrangement with Hallmark brought in still more money. But she seemed not to care: she was baffled when the first of her reproduction royalty checks arrived, and when Otto Kallir offered to pay her an additional sum for paintings Louis Caldor had bought from her early on and later sold at a considerable profit, she sent the check back, protesting that she had already been paid once, and fairly.

By the end of the 1940s Grandma Moses' paintings had been included in more than 65 exhibits, and she had had nearly 50 one-man shows. Her name was a now household word in America, and after the end of World War II her reputation had spread abroad as well. By the 1950s major American musuems were acquiring a "Grandma Moses" for their collections.

While she generally took little notice of her growing fame, some of its side-effects were inescapable. A film crew arrived in Eagle Bridge to make a documentary about her; Archibald MacLeish wrote the text and did the narration, and the film was nominated for an Academy Award. Colleges presented her with honorary degrees. In 1949 Grandma Moses went to Washington, DC, to receive the Women's National Press Club Award presented by President Harry S Truman before an audience that included Supreme Court Justices and Cabinet members. Grandma Moses was quite taken with President Truman, and he with her; at a private gathering the next day she even managed to persuade him to play a bit on the piano. Afterwards she she said tht he reminded her of one of her own boys.

For some years Otto Kallir had been urging Grandma Moses to write down her life story, and every now and then she would jot down some bits and pieces, some of which were assembled into magazine articles. Kallir arranged to have his assistant take dictation of her other memories, and in 1952 *Grandma Moses: My Life's History* was published. Only a fragment of the book dealt with her life after she had become famous. Mostly it was the story of her childhood and life as a young wife and mother, of the experiences that produced her prodigious outpouring of paintings. At the end of the book she reflected on her life from the perspective of some 90 years. "I wonder sometimes whether we are progressing. In my childhood days life was different . . . we were slower . . . we had a good and happy life . . . they don't take time to be happy nowadays. But when you come to big questions like that don't think too much, you must skip them

Left: "Eisenhower Farm," 1956. The president loved this Grandma Moses scene of his Gettysburg home.

Right: America's best-known primitive artist cuts her hundredth-birthday cake. Grandma Moses died the following year, 1961, at the age of 101.

. . . I look back on my life like a good day's work, it was done and I feel satisfied with it."

Grandma Moses wrote these autumnal lines in the early 1950s, but as it turned out, her life and her work were far from done. She had already painted hundreds of pictures, and at an age when many people are content just to reflect on their lives, she was still thinking about what she would do next. If she had not taken up painting, she wrote in *My Life's History*, she would have found something else to keep her busy – maybe raising chickens. "I would never sit back in a rocking chair, waiting for someone to help me."

Grandma Moses' work and no-nonsense ways were brought to a wide audience in 1955 when Edward R. Murrow interviewed her on his television program "See It Now." The camera crew filmed her painting one of her favorite subjects, sugaring off, and trying to cajole Murrow into trying his hand at painting too. But what was most striking was Grandma Moses' calm acceptance of what she felt life held in store for her. "What are you going to do for the next 20 years, Grandma Moses?" Murrow asked.

"I am going up yonder," she replied. "Naturally – naturally, I should. After you get to be about so old you can't expect to go on much further."

A bit taken aback by her frankness, Murrow countered, "But you don't spend much time thinking about it or worrying about it, do you?"

"Oh, no. No. No. You don't worry because you think, well, what a blessing it will be to be all united again. I'm the last one left of my sister and brothers."

But in the meantime Grandma Moses still had work to do. Even in her late 90s she kept on painting, and her pictures continue to be in demand. By the end of the 1950s her work was beginning to acquire an impressionist quality. Her colors were more muted, and the landscape forms had softer edges. But this

seemed less a diminishing of her powers than a refining of them.

On September 7, 1960, Grandma Moses turned 100. New York Governor Nelson Rockefeller proclaimed the date "Grandma Moses Day," and the little post office in Eagle Bridge was swamped with cards and gifts. In honor of Grandma Moses' hundredth birthday the IBM Corporation's Gallery of Arts and Sciences staged an exhibition of her works titled "My Life's History."

Shortly after she reached the century mark, Grandma Moses' health began to suffer. It was hard for her to get about, and now she seldom left her house, but she still did not give up her painting; on the contrary, it was a pleasure for her, a way of continuing to feel useful. And she had a new project: an assignment from Random House to illustrate Clement Moore's classic poem, "The Night Before Christmas." Grandma Moses began the paintings in March of 1960 and finished them in November. They were more abstract than her other works, with a large dose of whimsy that suited the subject. She showed expectant children "nestled all snug in their beds" beneath a colorful quilt in "Waiting for Santa Claus," and the jolly old man heading off into a star-studded deep blue night in "So Long till Next Year." Grandma Moses' version of "The Night Before Christmas" went on to become a classic Christmas book.

She would not live to see it in print, however. Early in 1961 she had several falls, and that July her sons brought her to a local nursing home for care. Grandma Moses loathed the place, and to make matters worse, she was deprived of her painting: for some unknown reason her doctor – the same doctor she had had for half a century – thought she would be better off if not painting. There were times when she was so annoyed with him that she would hide his stethoscope and refuse to reveal where it was unless he let her go back home. The painting titled "Rainbow," completed in June of 1961, just before she entered the nursing home, was in fact to be Grandma Moses' last.

She was in the home for her 101st birthday, and the scene was a repeat of the previous year's outpouring of cards and flowers and gifts from her admirers. But over the next several months her condition grew worse: she slept a good portion of every day and was becoming increasingly confused. Finally, on December 13, 1961, at the age of 101, Anna Mary Robertson Moses died. "She just wore out," her doctor said.

Grandma Moses' death was front-page news, and there were countless tributes to both her talents and the life she had led. *The New Yorker* magazine put her in the same class as Churchill and Schweitzer, calling her "one of those old people who make the world seem safer."

Grandma Moses' reputation in the art world suffered somewhat in the years immediately following her death, but time eventually proved kind to her, and her public popularity never flagged. In the 1960s the Bennington Museum's exhibits of her work were so well-received that the museum opened a Grandma Moses Gallery for several years. In 1969 her achievements were honored by a United States postage stamp. In 1985 a Grandma Moses retrospective toured six cities in the United States, and the critic for the *New York Times* wrote, "despite the fame and fortune that bore down on this talented woman . . . she weathered the storm very well."

Her secret, perhaps, was a deep-rooted sense of well-being, and the best of her paintings manage to evoke a similar feeling in those who see them. Even today, Grandma Moses' paintings continue to convey the pleasure she took in the world around her. Her message was a simple one. Life is good, and satisfying, and never dull.

The Spring in Evening, 1947. Oil
on pressed wood, 27×21 in. K
706

SEASONS AND CELEBRATIONS

"On a farm," Grandma Moses once reflected, " the days are nearly all the same, nothing changes but the seasons." Which was not to say that farm life was dull; as Grandma Moses saw it, every season held something special. And she had a talent for showing the side of an occasion that might escape a less keen observer.

Thus she might depict a side of Thanksgiving that was usually ignored: catching the turkey for the day's dinner. And it was the same in her paintings of other holidays. She got down to the basics, like the Christmas treks into the snowy woods to find a tree. No detail escaped her eye. "Country Fair," a painting of a much-anticipated event in the lives of farmers, is chock-full of life, from the chickens scratching about in the dirt to the peddler struggling to hang on to his bunch of balloons to the ferris wheel tucked away in a field.

She painted not only such big events in people's lives as weddings and homecomings, but the little ones as well. To Grandma Moses, even a day whiled away flying kites or playing games in the fields was an occasion to remember.

And her sense of humor was never far from the surface. "Halloween" shows a farm family getting ready for the holiday. There are barrels filled with apples for bobbing, men rolling in kegs of cider, jack-o-lanterns with happy faces – and two ghost-like figures racing through the scene.

When Random House asked Grandma Moses to illustrate "The Night Before Christmas" she hesitated before taking on the job; after a career based on painting only what she knew, it didn't seem quite right for her to embark on a project based on a made-up story. But she eventually changed her mind – she had always liked the poem, after all – and her "Night Before Christmas" pictures succeed in capturing all the excitement and anticipation of Clement Moore's poem.

But there is little doubt that she was more comfortable painting scenes she knew from her own experience. Sugaring off – boiling down the sap collected from maple trees into syrup – was one of Grandma Moses' favorite subjects, and given her memories of the job, it is little wonder. She and her brothers would race back and forth from the trees her father had tapped, keeping the pots filled with simmering syrup. When the job was done their reward was fresh syrup on buckwheat cakes and hot biscuits. Later came sugaring off parties, where, she once said, people would "eat their fill and go home to dream sweet dreams."

Winter scenes of sledding youngsters were another of Grandma Moses' perennial subjects. A bit of a tomboy as a child (if her brother climbed to the eave of the house, she once said, she'd go him one better and climb all the way to the peak), she relished winter races down snowy hills on home-made sleds. "We would go up a field above the orchard, get on our sleighs, and away we would go! Lester had a sleigh with cast iron runners, Horace had an old wash bench, upside down, but very safe, Arthur a dust pan, and I an old scoop shovel. Oh, what fun!"

There was no time of year Grandma Moses did not like, it seemed. Spring, she wrote, brings us "nearer to God's intentions, nearer to nature, free from the hubbub of life." In summer there was haying to be done and fruit and berries to be gathered, plus the excitement of the church picnic when "the children can have all the cake and lemonade they want, water melon and peanuts, what a wonderful treat!" Fall brought hard, satisfying work in preparation for the cold weather to come. And even winter held out promises, the chance to skate on icy lakes that looked like glass or to climb aboard a sleigh and burrow under warm blankets for a ride along snowy roads. Always, Grandma Moses' paintings seemed to say, life held something good in store if you knew where to look for it.

Fireboard, 1918. Oil on pressed
wood, 32¼×38¾ in. Private
collection K 1

All Dressed Up for Sunday, ca.
1940. Oil on pressed wood,
11¼×13 in. K 3

Thanksgiving Turkey, 1943. Oil on pressed wood, 15⅛×19⅛ in. K 293

The Lone Traveler, 1946. Oil on
pressed wood, 16×19¾ in. K
594

Bringing in the Yule Log, 1946.
Oil on pressed wood, 18×23 in.
K 589

Overleaf:
Christmas At Home, 1946. Oil
on pressed wood, 18×23 in. K
586

The Proposal, 1948. Oil on
masonite, 35×45¼ in. K 755

The Dividing of the Ways, 1947.
Oil on pressed wood, 16×20 in.
K 701

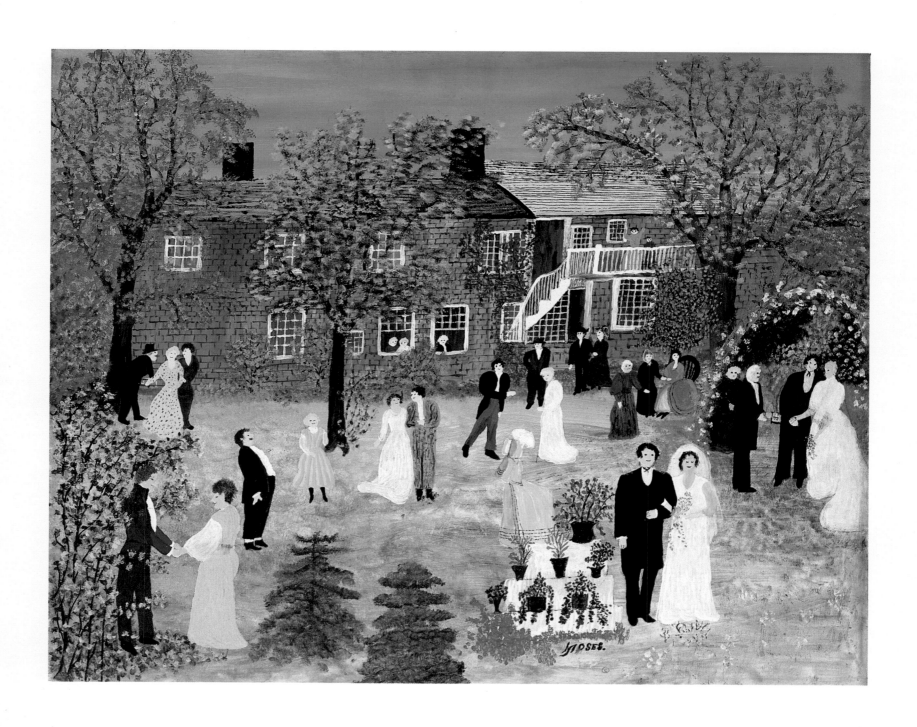

A Country Wedding, 1951. Oil
on pressed wood, 16½×21½ in.
K 968

July Fourth, 1951. Oil on pressed wood, 23⅞×30 in. K 999

Overleaf:
It Snows, Oh It Snows, 1951. Oil on pressed wood, 24×30 in. K 971

Home for Thanksgiving, 1952.
Oil on pressed wood, 18×24 in.
K 1062

Joy Ride, 1953. Oil on pressed
wood, 18×24 in. K 1079

Halloween, 1955. Oil on pressed
wood, 18×24 in. K 1188

Balloon, 1957. Oil on pressed
wood, 15⅞×24 in. K 1289

Overleaf:
The Lake, 1957. Oil on pressed
wood, 15⅞×23⅞ in. K 1279

Witches, 1960. Oil on pressed
wood, 16×24 in. Private
collection. K 1477

You Better Be Good, 1960. Oil on pressed wood, 12×16 in. K 1476

Overleaf:
Santa Claus, 1960. Oil on pressed wood, 16×24 in. Private collection. K 1455

Haying Time, 1945. Oil on
pressed wood, 24×30 in.
Private collection. K 485

COUNTRY LIFE

Grandma Moses' discovery as an artist came at just the right time: her homespun images of rural scenes were a welcome tonic for a nation just emerging from the Great Depression, caught up in the changes brought on by technology and on the brink of global war. Her paintings conjured up days when life was simple, and a major problem was how to snare a turkey for the Thanksgiving table. They managed to portray in a matter-of-fact way the essence of the country's strengths: hard work, a sense of community, a devotion to the land.

One of the keys to Grandma Moses' success was that she stuck to painting what she knew. Any farmer taking a look at one of her paintings, someone familiar with her work once said, would nod his head approvingly; the farms she painted were real farms, not some artistic generalization about them. But at the same time, her work was suffused with imagination. Grandma Moses had little use for painting "from life." She never set up her paints outdoors and seldom recorded an event as it was actually happening. Instead, the scenes that Grandma Moses painted had first to pass through the prism of her imagination or memory. She was inspired to paint her prize-winning "The Old Oaken Bucket" by recalling a story told to her by one of the women she had worked for as a girl. "Black Horses," one of her most acclaimed early paintings, depicts the mounts one of her ancestors was said to have ridden in the Revolutionary War. And Grandma Moses had certainly lived through enough church picnics, skating parties and country fairs to provide her with grist for dozens of paintings.

Nothing was as satisfying to Grandma Moses as hard work, it seemed, and life on a farm offered plenty of that. She even took pride in doing the laundry. There were no washing machines in her younger days, of course, and wash day was a major production: water had to be hauled from the spring, and then all the paraphernalia – the wash bench, tubs, scrub boards and pails – had to be set up before the actual washing could begin. She and her mother would start the job early in the day. "And a large, snow-white wash would be floating on the wind by eleven o'clock, if we were not lazy folks."

A look at the titles of her paintings gives a good idea of what life on a nineteenth- or early twentieth-century farm entailed: the horses being shod, the wagons being fixed, the fields being plowed, the crops being harvested. In the country much of the work was shared, and much of it doubled as a social occasion as well. Grandma Moses painted pictures of quilting bees that showed the women busy stitching while the men and children kept occupied until it was time to eat. She painted pictures of men roofing a barn, their white shirts setting them off from the greens and browns of the barn and surrounding fields and hills. She painted minor events, such as the mailman's arrival, and managed to make them seem significant.

And she took note of the changing times in a tongue-in-cheek kind of way. In paintings like "The First Automobile" she let people know just how she felt about the new machine. Black, angular, and just slightly menacing, the car stands in stark contrast to the lovely blossoming trees that flower by the edge of the road.

There was always something going on in Grandma Moses' world, and always a story to be told. However simple life may be, her paintings glowingly attest, it need never be boring.

The First Automobile, 1944. Oil
on pressed wood, 9¾×11½ in.
K 6

Mary and Little Lamb, 1947. Oil
on masonite, 24×34½ in. K
650

Apple Butter Making, 1947. Oil
on pressed wood, 16½×23⅝ in.
Private collection. K 653

The Mailman Has Gone, 1949.
Oil on pressed wood,
16¾×21½ in. K 818

Overleaf:
Country Fair, 1950. Oil on
canvas, 35×45. K 921

The Barn Dance, 1950. Oil on canvas, 35×45. K 920

Barn Roofing, 1951. Oil on
pressed wood, 18×24 in. K 986

Husking Bee, 1951. Oil on
pressed wood, 19×24 in. K 987

Overleaf:
Busy Street, 1952. Oil on
pressed wood, 18×24 in. K
1054

Maple Bush, 1953. Oil on masonite, 12×18 in. K 1088

Overleaf:
Wagon Repair Shop, 1960. Oil on pressed wood, 16×24 in. K 1478

Rockabye, 1957. Oil on pressed
wood, 11⅞×16 in. K 1303

At Home

When she was a little girl Grandma Moses would head out to the orchards, gather up a pile of stones and build herself a little house, complete with pantry shelves stocked with whatever broken dishes she could get her hands on. With a young friend, she would play there for hours. Home, whether it was real or imagined, was a wonderful place to her.

Her hectic trip to New York City in 1941 to speak at Gimbels department store was one of the few times she ventured from her cozy world. Two years later she painted "Grandma Going to the Big City," and there is no mistaking her feelings about the occasion. Grandma Moses sits in a carriage in the foreground of the picture, surrounded by her family and friends; little children gaily wave goodbye. But dark clouds hang overhead, and in the distance, past the tranquil lake and trees and hills, looms a faceless city. The message is clear: "There's no place like home."

Her trip to Washington, DC, in 1949, when she met President Truman, seems to have been more enjoyable for her, but she was still glad to get home. More than 800 people – twice the population of Eagle Bridge – turned out to welcome her back; the high school band played, the children sang and she was presented with flowers. But when it was over, Grandma Moses said, "In a way I was glad to get back and go to bed that night."

Throughout her career Grandma Moses was fond of painting old homesteads of local repute. Some, like the house of her great-great-grandfather, Hezekiah King, lived only through her pictures; the house itself had burned to the ground in 1800, and Grandma Moses had to imagine how it must have looked. The Old Checkered House, one of her most popular subjects, was a local landmark, one of those "old-time homes," Grandma Moses said, that were "going fast." Demand for Checkered House paintings was so great that she painted nearly two dozen versions of it. Some of the paintings showed the house as Grandma Moses imagined it at the time it was built, in the 1700s; others depicted it as it might have looked 50 or 100 years later. She painted it from several different angles, in winter and summer. Otto Kallir once asked Grandma Moses how she could keep painting the same subject and still manage to come up with something fresh. The answer was simple, she replied; all she had to do was imagine that she was looking out on a scene from the right side of her window, or from the left, and the elements of entirely different compositions would fall into place.

President Dwight D. Eisenhower was a fan of Grandma Moses, and when he was about to complete his third year in office his Cabinet members looked about for a suitable gift to mark the occasion. They settled on commissioning Grandma Moses to paint a picture of the Eisenhower farm in Gettysburg, Pennsylvania. Though she had never seen the farm, Grandma Moses agreed to paint it, and equipped with an assortment of black and white photographs, she set to work. The finished painting pleased President Eisenhower greatly. Grandma Moses had added her own characteristic touches: the Eisenhower grandchildren riding along in a horse-drawn cart, a lively little dog in the foreground, as well as some embellishments that the president found amusing: a grander herd of cattle than he actually had, for example, and a putting green of impressive proportions. Thus had Grandma Moses managed not only to portray the president's home but to capture something of the love and pride it inspired in him.

Grandma Moses painted hundreds of homes over the course of her career. There were pictures of the house she lived in as a child, her homes in the Shenandoah Valley, her father's house, her grandfather's house, her daughter's house in Vermont – in all probability, every home she ever knew. And not one of them is less than inviting.

The Shepherd Comes Home from
the Hills, n.d. Worsted,
12½×27½ in. Bennington
Museum, Bennington, VT. K
37W

Overleaf:
Back Yard at Home, 1940. Oil
on pressed wood, 12×16½ in.
Private collection. K 7

Above:
My Hills of Home, 1941. Oil on
pressed wood, 17¾×36 in. K
99

Right:
Old Checkered House, 1944. Oil
on pressed wood, 24×43 in. K
367

Over the River to Grandma's House, 1944. Oil on pressed wood, 19¼×33¼ in. K 368

In the Studio, 1944. Oil on
pressed wood, 18×23½ in. K
461

Wash Day. 1945. Oil on pressed wood, 17¾×23½ in. Museum of Art, Rhode Island School of Design; Gift of Mrs. Murray S. Danforth. K 498

*Grandma Moses' Childhood
Home*, 1946. Oil on pressed
wood, 36×48 in. K 575

Hoosick Valley (from the Window), 1946. Oil on pressed wood, 19½×22 in. K 611

A Tramp on Christmas Day,
1946. Oil on pressed board,
16×19⅞ in. K 595

Taking in Laundry, 1951. Oil on
pressed wood, 17×21¾ in. K
967

Overleaf:
Checkered House, 1955. Oil on
pressed wood, 18×24 in. K
1165

Old Times, 1957. Oil on pressed
wood, 16×24 in. K 1296

In the Park, 1944. Oil on
canvas, 36×45 in. K 343

THE LAND

Grandma Moses always loved to paint the land, even in her earliest attempts at the "lambscapes" about which her brothers used to tease her. When she decorated her little tip-up table in 1918 she did not paint people, but trees and skies. Her first "big" painting, the parlor fireboard, was a landscape.

She was never very successful in portraying people – they were often awkward and sometimes little more than stick figures – and even at the height of her success as an artist she admitted that she never felt she got her interiors quite right. But Grandma Moses' talents were ideally suited for painting the land around her, and pictures of the land she knew, from the Shenandoah Valley of Virginia to the Hoosick Valley of New York, make up the bulk of her work.

During her butter-making days in Virginia, years before she started painting in earnest, Grandma Moses would while away the time at the churn by gazing out on the Shenandoah Valley and wishing she could paint a picture of the scene. When she finally was able to, it was obvious that she had stored away almost every little detail. Highly decorative, in the mode of the primitive painters with whom Grandma Moses was often grouped, her landscapes did more than present hills and valleys and trees and fields; they told stories as well, or inspired the viewer to make them up. Hidden away in a corner of one landscape there might be a hunter aiming his gun. In another, a cow pasture would be set off by the figures of a pair of young children deep in conversation in the foreground. In yet another, a vista of faraway hills would be balanced by a farmer steering a horse-drawn plow and a small boy climbing a tree.

The "Grandma Moses look," her knack of somehow managing to merge a wide variety of elements into a harmonious whole, is best displayed in her landscapes. This ability to infuse equal vitality into both foregrounds and backgrounds has eluded many artists far better trained than she, and even she, gifted as she was, had to work at it. One day, she recalled, she happened to look out at a car parked near her house, and in its hubcap she saw a reflection of just the effect she had been searching for: one that encompassed every detail and gave each a balanced importance.

In *My Life's History* Grandma Moses tells of an animated discussion with her brother Arthur about what heaven would be like. Arthur thought that heaven must be filled with lots of good things to eat. Young Anna Mary saw it differently: for her, heaven would be a place overflowing with flowers. Most of her landscapes convey that sunny outlook with their bright colors and pleasing proportions.

To be sure, there were times when she saw the land in a different light. In paintings like "The Dead Tree," with its ominously stark white tree standing apart from its surroundings, she transformed the land into a place of drama. In other paintings she showed storms coming, or fires raging. But more often Grandma Moses' land was a gentle place. She balanced rolling hills with curving rows of trees in paintings like "Hoosick Valley," and set off the patchwork fields in the distance of "Cambridge" with a cluster of houses in the middle of the painting and a pair of men and horses in the foreground.

Untrained as a painter, she had little knowledge of perspective, but that lack never detracts from her landscapes; instead, it enhances their charm. By focussing attention on several elements in a scene, she was able to give her landscapes a kind of psychological or narrative depth fully as effective as hypothetical horizon lines and vanishing-points.

Grandma Moses' fondness for painting the countryside she knew so well never waned. Her very last painting, "Rainbow," was another landscape.

Home Among the Snow Hills,
1942. Oil on pressed wood,
8×10 in. K 135

Hoosick Valley, 1942. Oil on
pressed wood, 15¼×20½ in. K
174

Missouri, 1943. Oil on pressed
wood, 20×23¾ in. K 224

Old Oaken Bucket in Winter,
1944. Oil on pressed wood,
20×33 in. K 351

The Old Oaken Bucket, 1947.
Oil on masonite, 23½×27½ in.
K 669

The Dead Tree, 1948. Oil on
pressed wood, 16×20 in. K 792

Hoosick Falls, New York, in Winter, 1944. Oil on pressed wood, 20×24 in. K 425

The Flag, 1958. Oil on pressed
wood, 12×16 in. K 1369

The Spillway, 1954. Oil on
pressed wood, 18×24 in. K
1141.

Spotted Horses, 1950. Oil on
pressed wood, 16×19 in. K 908

The Rainbow, 1951. Oil on pressed wood, 19⅞×23⅞ in. Private collection. K 1004

Overleaf:
Corn, 1958. Oil on pressed wood, 16×23⅞ in. K 1362

Pages 110-111:
Eagle Bridge Hotel, 1959. Oil on pressed wood, 16×24 in. K 1387

LIST OF COLOR PLATES

Picture Credits

All photos, unless otherwise noted, are copyrighted by the Grandma Moses Properties Company. All transparencies were provided by Galerie St. Etienne, NY.

Grandma Moses Properties: 6(photograph by Ifor Thomas), 7(both), 8, 9, 10, 13, 16(*Eisenhower Home*, 1956, Oil on pressed wood, 16×24″, K. 1204).

UPI/Bettmann Newsphotos: 11, 12, 14, 15, 17.

Acknowledgments

The publisher would like to thank the following people who helped in the preparation of this book: Don Longabucco, who designed it; Rita Longabucco, who did the picture research; and John Kirk, who edited the text.